EXPOUNDING THE ARTS

By Douglas C. Mason

From research prepared for:

The Adam Smith Institute

1987

1940

P U (DIAS)

CONTENTS

First published in the UK in 1987 by
ASI (Research) Ltd, London SWlP 3DJ
(c) Adam Smith Institute, 1987

ISBN 1 870109 05 8

Printed in Great Britain by Imediacopy Limited, London SW1

1. INTRODUCTION: The Growth of Subsidised Culture

Like Topsy, state support for artistic activity just "grow'd."

As long ago as 1700, the Government acquired Sir Robert Cotton's books. In 1753 it purchased Sir Hans Sloane's collection and used it, along with the Cotton library and other donations, to form the nucleus of what was later to become the British Museum. Subsequent state acquisitions included the Elgin Marbles in 1816 and the Angerstein collection in 1824.

While the British Museum was established by Act of Parliament, other national museums and galleries had differing origins. The National Gallery, for example, was set up by a Treasury Minute in 1824 while the National Galleries of Scotland developed under the control of the Board of Trustees for Manufactures, established under Acts of 1726 governing Scotland's fisheries, linen and hemp industries.

The Victoria and Albert Museum was founded using the £200,000 profit on the Great Exhibition of 1851, attended by six and a half million paying visitors.

Schools of design were first established in 1836 by the Board of Trade. By 1849 there were sixteen of them. In 1857, the first Schools of Art were founded. By 1863 there were ninety.

Increasing government involvement in artistic activity was recognised by the formation in 1851, within the Board of Trade, of the Department of Practical Art. Two years later it became the Department of Science and Art and was taken over by the Education Department in 1856, eventually to re-emerge as the Office of Arts and Libraries in 1979.

Where public funding was regarded as appropriate both for national museums and galleries and for education, it was not so considered for the performing arts. Some subsidies were paid for film-making from 1916 and three payments were made to Covent Garden in the 1930s but there was no significant or consistent support for the performing arts from public funds until the Second World War.

Serious central government involvement in historic buildings and monuments dates only from the late nineteenth century. The Ancient Monuments Protection Act of 1882 provided that a list of monuments should be made and gave powers to the Commissioners of Works to accept custody of such sites from their owners. Sixty-eight prehistoric sites were listed. Subsequent legislation increased those powers and extended them to local authorities. In 1908, for example, Royal Commissions were established to draw up an inventory of the ancient and historic monuments of England, Scotland and Wales.

In 1895, the National Trust was formed with statutory powers to promote the preservation, particularly through acquisition, of places of historic interest and natural beauty and hold them in trust for the nation.

The government's powers over monuments passed in time from the Commissioners of Works to the Ministry of Public Buildings and Works and in due course to the Department of the Environment and the Scottish and Welsh Offices.

Local government growth

The 1845 Museums of Art in Corporate Towns Act first allowed local authorities to use the rates to support cultural activity although some municipal corporations had been sponsoring, organising or supporting cultural events of one sort or another for a century or so before.

Subsequent legislation widened the powers to include libraries. With the aid, often, of local benefactors, substantial development of municipal museums, art galleries, and concert halls took place from the 1880s. By the outbreak of the Second World War there were around 400 local authority museums and galleries and roughly half that number of municipal theatres.

In 1931 the Standing Commission on Museums and Galleries was established to give advice at both national and local level. It subsequently also became a channel for providing central government support to local authorities.

Where central government opposed the use of taxpayers' money to support cultural activity, it did continue to provide some powers to local government. In the interests of public health, for example, legislation in the late nineteenth and early twentieth century allowed councils to support open air concerts. A few towns also obtained their own special powers by private Acts of Parliament. Bournemouth, for example, established its own municipal symphony orchestra in this way in 1894.

The legacy of war

It was during and after the Second World War that attitudes towards public funding of the performing arts began to change. The need to entertain troops and civilians led to the formation of a number of organisations, funded by the taxpayer, which organised various kinds of concerts. The largest was ENSA, the Entertainment National Service Association, but it was the smaller Council for the Encouragement of Music and the Arts, intended to bring music and subsequently theatre to war workers, that survived to be transformed, in 1945, into the Arts Council.

Although the subsidies paid through it in the early post war years were small, the principle of permanent public funding was established. Today it has grown to the point where it is now generally assumed that "the arts", however defined, cannot be

expected to survive and flourish without regular, guaranteed and increasing subsidies from both the taxpayer and the ratepayer.

Underlying virtually all current discussion of arts funding is the belief that 'the arts' could not attract sufficient audiences willing to pay realistic ticket prices to be able to pay their way; that opera, ballet or serious music would not be performed; that paintings would not be painted; that good poetry and serious literature would not be written or published; that new plays would not be written or performed.

It is widely accepted that the public must be compelled through taxation and rates to support those arts activities which they would not willingly support through their own expenditure.

It is even argued by some that the very effort of attempting to attract audiences might well undermine artistic integrity.

Throughout most of the postwar era, such views have not been widely challenged. And those who did dare to question them faced the accusations from the arts lobby that they were somehow inferior because they did not appreciate the higher things in life. They were insultingly dismissed as philistines and their arguments were ignored.[1]

Anyone who suggested that the arts should be expected to pay their way was accused, misusing Oscar Wilde's words, of knowing "the price of everything and the value of nothing."[2]

In such a climate, it is scarcely surprising that the arts have benefited from a comfortable, bi-partisan benevolence, backed up by regular subsidies from the public purse. Radical theatre companies might arouse protest from those whose political views they offend. Individual "works of art" might depart so far from the accepted norms that they are dismissed as worthless. But there has been general agreement that the arts were desirable in themselves and merited largely uncritical financial support.

Political debate has usually been limited to the Opposition disagreeing with the Government only to the extent of suggesting that their grant in aid to the Arts Council was not large enough.
----
[1] Like the Vandals, the Philistines had a sad history. No different from other minor mediterranean peoples, they made the mistake of falling out with the Israelites. From that inauspicious beginning there was no turning back. Following fatal riots in 1689, the students at Jena applied the Old Testament condemnations to the townspeople. Other German students followed suit and, subsequently, Matthew Arnold introduced the insult to Britain, particularly in his book, Culture and Anarchy.
[2] Wilde was actually describing a "cynic" rather than someone lacking in cultural appreciation, a fact which suggests that those who use the phrase may themselves be less knowledgable about literature than they would like to pretend.

3

Today that cosy consensus is breaking down. While public funding of the arts still commands majority support in all political parties, the degree and nature of that support, the way it is given and, indeed, the kind of arts to which it should be given are all subject to challenge and debate. And, underlying that debate, are fundamental disagreements concerning the purpose of art and the justification for spending public money in its support.

In 1978, Sir Roy Shaw, the then Secretary General of the Arts Council, warned that "it would be disastrous if arts policy, which has hitherto been almost fully bi-partisan, ever became a political football to be kicked to right or left with every change of government."[3]

By the very growth in their public funding, by their insistence on even greater increases, and sometimes by their own artistic policies, the subsidised arts have become just such a political football. It is towards developing a new arts policy that would insulate the arts from political interference that this report is aimed.

[3] 33rd. Annual Report and Accounts (London: Arts Council 1978, page 7)

2. ARTS SUPPORT TODAY: Breaking the Billion Pound Barrier

Central government funding for the arts and heritage comes from several departments, the principal ones being the Office of Arts and Libraries, the Department of the Environment, the Department of Education and Science, the Treasury, and the Scottish, Welsh and Northern Ireland Offices. Table 1 gives the readily identifiable items of expenditure for each of them.

Table 1A   Planned expenditure on arts and heritage 1987-88 (£m)

Office of Arts and Libraries	
Museums and Galleries	80.478
Building and maintenance(a)	30.000
Arts Council	138.401
British Films Institute, etc.	11.157
Crafts Council	2.022
Research and Surveys	0.201
International organisations, etc.	0.021
Business Sponsorship incentive scheme	1.750
Arts Marketing Scheme	0.250
Government Indemnity Scheme	0.150
Government Art Collection	0.161
National Heritage Memorial Fund	1.500
Assets accepted in lieu of tax	1.000
Department of the Environment	
Environmental Initiative	1.500
European Year of the Environment	0.300
Incentive award scheme for Art and Architecture	0.060
Royal Palaces and Royal Parks	10.120
Historic Buildings and Monuments Commission	64.850
Buildings and maintenance(a)	20.000
Board of Trustees of the Armouries	3.000
Redundant Churches Fund	0.950
National Heritage Memorial Fund	1.560
Assets Accepted in lieu of tax	1.000
Royal Commission on Historic Monuments	3.400
International organisations	0.082
Royal Fine Arts Commission	0.140
Department of Education and Science	
Grants to music and ballet schools	3.441
Royal College of Art	7.499
British Museum (Natural History)	17.558

Note:(a) Estimated proportions of the expenditure relating to museums, galleries and the heritage incurred by the Property Services Agency on behalf of the department.
Source: Supply Estimates 1987-88 (HC 227-XIII London: HMSO 1987)

Table 1B   Planned expenditure on arts and heritage 1987-88 (£m)

The Treasury

        Assets accepted in lieu of tax (contingency)   10.000

Scottish Office
        Scottish Film Council   0.496
        Scottish Film Production Fund   0.072
        Grants to cultural organisations   0.250
        National Museums of Scotland   5.017
        National Galleries of Scotland   3.417
        Scottish Museums Council   0.440
        Historic buildings and ancient monuments   9.850
        Buildings and maintenance(a)   7.493
        Royal Fine Arts Commission for Scotland   0.103
        Grants to local authorities for conservation   0.332
        Grants to other bodies   0.523

Welsh Office
        Historic buildings and ancient monuments   5.423
        National Museums of Wales   12.504
        Council of Museums in Wales   0.300
        Arts feasibility studies   0.050

Northern Ireland Office
        Arts Council of Northern Ireland   3.477
        Museums   4.256
        Historic buildings and ancient monuments   3.1

Note:(a) Expenditure incurred by the Property Services Agency and
charged to the department. Perhaps £5 million relates to museums
and galleries.
Source: Supply Estimates 1987-88, various written parliamentary
answers, and information from the Northern Ireland Departments of
Education and the Environment.

To the above has to be added the appropriate share of each
departments administrative expenditure. It must be noted, too,
that there is significant other expenditure that is not readily
identifiable. Substantial amounts are spent on arts related
education at all levels.[4] Few of the grants paid to voluntary
organisations are separately identified unless the information is
subsequently sought in a parliamentary question. Other support is
given indirectly through government agencies. Payments from the
University Grants Committee, for example, go in part to support
university museums, galleries, arts centres and other arts and
heritage spending.

In addition to the departments detailed above, the Ministry of
Defence maintains six service museums at a net cost of £4.790
----
[4]   In 1986/87, for example, the Scottish Office alone spent
       £18.791 million maintaining three colleges of art and the
       Royal Scottish Academy of Music and Drama.

million along with more than a hundred regimental and corps museums. It spends something of the order of £45 million on military bands including maintaining three schools of music.

The Foreign Office spends £133,000 supporting conferences, artistic performances and other cultural activities and, through its payment of £55.658 million to the British Council and £116.500 million towards the external services of the BBC, contributes further significant sums towards arts related activities.[5]

The Department of Trade and Industry pays £4.555 to the Design Council, £1.500 million to British Screen Finance, Ltd., £30,000 to the British Fashion Council and has £500,000 available for loans and grants towards film development and production. The Department of Energy has even made payments towards scripts for plays that featured energy efficiency messages.

A wide range of government agencies, other than those sponsored by the departments mentioned above, provide financial support towards arts and heritage activity. The BBC plays a major role, though without using taxpayer's money. The Manpower Services Commission estimates that it spent £21 million directly last year along with another £9 million for arts related small business ventures through the Enterprise Allowance Scheme.[6] Its efforts have attracted the criticism that in some areas it spends as much on the arts as the regional arts associations but without the ability to assess the quality of what is being produced.

The Property Services Agency makes modest provision for the purchase of works of art to be incorporated in new buildings it erects. The British Tourist Authority, along with the English, Scottish, Welsh and Northern Ireland Tourist Boards, contribute from time to time to arts, heritage and other culture related projects. So, too, do the various development agencies such as the Development Commission, the Councils for Small Industries in Rural Areas, the Scottish Development Agency, the Highlands and Islands Development Board, the Welsh Development Agency, the Development Board for Rural Wales, and the Industrial Development Board for Northern Ireland.

Figures for arts and heritage expenditure by local authorities in the various parts of the United Kingdom are not published in a consistent or readily usable form.[7] Nonetheless, attempts have been made over a number of years to produce figures for England and Wales and, for 1982/3, in Scotland.[8] These suggest that local government is spending only a little less than the Office
----
[5]   In 1983/84 the amount was estimated at £4.8 million (Facts
       About The Arts 2, Table 1:6)
[6]   Written parliamentary answer (Hansard 9th March 1987
       col. 18)
[7]   Facts About The Arts 2 (London: Policy Studies Institute
       1986, pages 11 to 13)
[8]   Ibid. (Tables 1:8 and 1:14)

of Arts and Libraries.

All of the above indicates that public support towards the arts and heritage will well exceed one billion pounds in 1987/88.

3. QUANGO CULTURE: Administering the Arts

AIDING THE ARTS

Government support for the arts is largely channelled through the Arts Council of Great Britain, formed in 1945 and given a Royal Charter a year later. It developed from the Council for the Encouragement of Music and the Arts, a body established at the start of the Second World War with money from the Pilgrim Trust and the Government to co-ordinate the provision of drama to war workers living in hostels and camps.

Its aims are "developing greater knowledge, understanding and practice of the fine arts exclusively, and in particular to increase the accessibility of the fine arts to the public...to improve the standard of execution of the fine arts and to advise and co-operate with...Government Departments, Local Authorities and other bodies on any matters concerning directly or indirectly with those objects..."

The Scottish and Welsh Arts Councils and, following the abolition of the Greater London Council, the South Bank Board are all committees of the Arts Council, from whom they receive their finance.

A sister body, the Arts Council of Northern Ireland, on the other hand, is a separate and independent organisation with a budget for 1987/88 of £3.477 million.

The Arts Council devolves part of its responsibilities to twelve English regional arts associations, originally set up following the Arts Council's withdrawal from the provision of its own regional offices. They co-ordinate support for local arts organisations from the Arts Council, the local authorities and business sponsors. On average, however, 70% of their money comes from the Arts Council.

The government grant to the Arts Council has grown from less than a quarter of a million pounds in 1945 to £135 million today. The way it plans to spend that grant during 1987-88 is shown in Table 2.

From the start, the Arts Council has seen its role as supporting professional work in certain areas of the arts. Choral music, for example, generally falls outside its normal funding criterion although choirs which are members of the National Federation of Music Societies can apply to Regional Arts Associations for support. The National Federation, itself, receives money from the Scottish Arts Council to support its members north of the border.

Little support has been given to amateur artists. While claiming

to encourage the development of the arts, the Arts Council has adopted the inherently contradictory policy of denying support, to amateur activities, particularly the National Youth Theatre, the National Youth Orchestra and similar organisations.

Table 2   Arts Council budgeted expenditure 1987-88 (£m)

England:	Art	3.840	
	Combined Arts	1.119	
	Dance	10.830	
	Drama	26.394	
	Film, Video and Broadcasting	0.448	
	Literature	0.546	
	Music	23.100	
	Touring	7.608	
	Regional Arts Associations	27.473	
	Planning/Development	0.903	
	Marketing and Resources	0.140	
	Administration and Operational	4.719	
	Contingency	0.361	
	Less met from reserves	(1.000)	
	Sub-total for England		106.481
Scotland:	Music, Opera and Dance	7.123	
	Drama	2.847	
	Art and Film	1.189	
	Literature	0.579	
	Combined Arts	1.537	
	Administration and Operational	0.914	
	Unallocated	0.051	
	Less met from reserves	(0.120)	
	Sub-total for Scotland		14.120
Wales:	Music, Opera and Dance	2.800	
	Drama	1.828	
	Art and Film	0.642	
	Literature	0.646	
	Arts Associations, Centres, etc.	1.113	
	Administration and Operational	0.823	
	Unallocated	0.028	
	Sub-total for Wales		7.880
Housing the Arts			1.161
South Bank Board			8.758

			138.400

Source: <u>Supply</u> <u>Estimates</u> <u>1987-88</u>

The bulk of Arts Council funding goes to providing more than a thousand grants, varying in size from over thirteen million pounds for the Royal Opera House down to much smaller amounts for some of the less well known local theatre companies.

A small amount goes to single project grants. When these were reviewed in 1985 it was estimated that it cost £500 to reach a decision on each such award.

Pressure groupings

Unfortunately, The Arts Council has not been content to carry out its appointed task of distributing public money on behalf of the taxpayer to artistic organisations. Instead, it has assumed the additional role of a campaigner for the arts. Its current chairman, Sir William Rees-Mogg, for example, sees the council as "a servant of the arts".[9]

It has joined with its clients in complaining that not enough money is given to the arts. It has supported them in prophesying disaster as in 1978 when it warned that the failure to provide more public money would lead to "the gradual deterioration of the financial health of most of our clients." [10]

In that year, its Secretary-General claimed that what any Minister for the Arts needed was the backing of informed opinion in support of the arts. "It is disappointing," he wrote, "that many of our clients do not realise that they have a part to play in presenting to politicians and the public the case for a general increase in arts subsidy."[11]

It would appear that his plea was heeded. The arts today are increasingly surrounded by a coterie of pressure groups dedicated to opposing any change in the existing funding arrangements, save for as large an increase as possible in the actual amount to be provided from taxes and rates.

The National Campaign for the Arts argues that the arts are paying for themselves, making the misleading claim that they pay more in value added tax than the Arts Council receives in cash (see Chapter 5). It publishes a quarterly newsletter campaigning for greater government subsidies.

SALVO, the Scottish Arts Lobby, claims to be supported by the majority of the major recipients of Arts Council cash in Scotland. Perhaps unconciously admitting a lack of public support, its adopted aim is to support and promote the arts to local and central government along with business in the public and private sectors.

The Free Access to Museums Campaign, established by a handful of local authorities and trade unions, sets out to defend the principle of free access to the core collection of museums and galleries although it accepts the justification for charging for special exhibitions or collections.

Such groups appear to receive little or no support from ordinary people whose interests they claim to be representing. Most
----
[9] 40th Annual Report and Accounts (London: Arts Council 1985, Page 2)
[10] 33rd. Annual Report and Accounts (London: Arts Council 1978, Page 8)
[11] Ibid. (Page 9)

finance seems to come from arts organisations, seeking increased public funding for their own activities, or from the more traditional pressure group backers in local government and the trade unions.

Expanding the arts

Nor is the arts lobby content to campaign for bigger subsidies. Concerned, no doubt, that the public might realise the extent to which they are being asked to subsidise the enjoyment of a tiny minority of the public, they try to define the arts in the widest possible sense, including very substantial areas of activity that do not get, and never have received, public subsidies.

Speaking in Parliament, the then Shadow Minister for the Arts, Norman Buchan, said: "Let us look at the scale of the arts. About 200,000 to 250,000 people are in broadcasting. About 200,000 people are in printing, the press and publication -- the written word. About 70,000 are involved in the popular music industry -- in recording, as artists, producers and so on." [12]

His successor as Shadow Minister, Mark Fisher, went even further, stating that "the arts today encompass publishing, broadcasting, radio, television, video, film, fashion, design, and the new technologies of satellite and cable." In response to a question he added photography to the list.[13]

The Arts Council have attempted to use an expanded definition of the arts to claim increased support. In his 1978 report, the Chairman referred to "the plain duty of government, both national and local, to stimulate more facilities for leisure activity of all kinds which must include a wider availability of the arts in general and easier access to them for all our people." [14]

In 1983, they claimed that the public spent a fifth of their income on the arts. To achieve that figure, however, they included money spent on books and the cinema as well as the live arts.

Even the government is guilty of claiming the achievement of commercial companies as a success for the arts. In the House of Commons, the Minister for the Arts, Richard Luce, used as "evidence of expansion and growth in the arts" the fact that "export sales of British books are over £340 million annually and royalties to British Record companies from abroad are estimated at $500 million."[15]

Underlying all such lobbying is an arrogant belief that those involved know better than the man in the street what is good for
----
[12] Hansard 20th June 1986 Col 1360
[13] Hansard 12th March 1987 Col. 503
[14] 33rd. Annual Report and Accounts (London: Arts Council 1978, Page 6)
[15] Hansard 12th March 1987 Col 492

him and what kind of art he ought to enjoy. His failure to consume the subsidised culture on offer is put down to a lack of education.

This kind of elitist nonsense was well stated by Sir Roy Shaw in his last report as Secretary General of the Arts Council. "So it seems plain that the main reason why the arts seem irrelevant to ordinary working people (who constitute just over half the population) is not that the arts are bourgeois, not that the people are different creatures from middle class people, but simply...that they have been conditioned by their inadequate education and their environment."[16]

And thus, in a kind of curious self-sufficient circular system, the Arts Council spends taxpayers' money to make the arts available to ordinary people and then spends even more of that money to try and persuade people to like the subsidised arts they are offered.

FUNDING FILMS

Some support towards film making is provided through the Arts Council but, traditionally, the greatest part of the industry's limited public subsidy has come through other agencies.

Table 3   Government support for the film industry 1987-88 (£m)

Office of Arts and Libraries	
British Film Institute	10.030
National Film and TV School	1.127
Department of Trade and Industry	
Grants to British Screen Finance Ltd.	1.500
Loans/grants for film development projects	0.500
Scottish Office	
Scottish Film Council	0.496
Scottish Film Production Fund	0.072

Note: Payments are also made through the Arts Council network, amounting in 1986/87 to more than half a million pounds.
Source: Supply Estimates 1987-88

Following radical changes in 1985, the Eady Levy, a long standing system of taxing cinemas on every seat they sold to provide support to British films, was ended. The National Film Finance Corporation, which had used part of the income from that levy to finance new film making, was converted into a private company, British Screen Finance Ltd., with continuing support from the taxpayer and new support from private sector film, television and video interests.

The new company was given the rights to the films its predecessor had helped to finance, providing an income of "not less than
----
[16] 38th Annual Report and Accounts (London: Arts Council 1983, Page 8)

13

£200,000 a year" with the potential to yield "considerably more for the next few years."[17] State involvement remains through an grant of £1.5 million plus the provision of finance to support work at the earliest stages of preparing a film project.

While that support comes from the Department of Trade and Industry, the Office of Arts and Libraries provides around two thirds of the running costs of the British Film Institute and half the costs of the National Film and Television School, the remainder coming from BBC, ITV and the film industry. Other support, as Table 3 shows, comes from the Scottish Office.

The British Film Institute has some limited involvement in Film Making but is principally involved in maintaining Britain's film archives and providing films to a network of regional theatres. Audiences, however, are relatively small, rising from 1.294 million in 1984 to 1.367 million in 1985.

PRESERVING THE HERITAGE

Where public support for the arts is largely channelled through one body, conservation of Britain's heritage, whether in museums, galleries, and historic houses, or as original buildings and ancient monuments, is shared among many ministries, councils, quangos and private individuals and organisation.

Table 4	Britain's museums and galleries
National museums and galleries	41
Local authority museums and galleries	658
University Museums(a)	21
Independent museums	1,250
Total(b)	1,961

Notes: (a) The total number is significantly greater if separate museums within a single university are taken into account.
(b) excluding historic houses and regimental or corps museums.
Source: Facts About the Arts 2

The very concept of a museum has changed significantly over post-war years. In the words of the Judges' Committee of the Museum of the Year award, "today it is much more of a 'broad church' embracing heritage centres, specialist museums...as well as the traditional collection based museums."[18]

That change has been accompanied by a remarkable growth in the number of museums with the total doubling over the past fifteen years. One new museum opens every fortnight. Table 4 gives an indication of the total numbers in 1986.
----
[17] Film Policy (Cmnd. 9319, London: HMSO 1984)
[18] Fourteenth Report of the Judges' Committee, printed in Museums and Galleries 1987 (East Grinstead: British Leisure Publications, 1986)

The audience for museums and galleries is changing, too. As the Judges' Committee went on to observe, "increased leisure is no doubt a factor behind the rapid mushrooming of museums: the audience for them world wide is larger, and growing faster than the audience for football. The directors are changing their attitudes to the public. The designers are transforming the old simple presentation concepts."[18]

Table 5 shows the numbers attending national and local authority museums and galleries but a national survey of more than 2,000 museums and galleries, both public and private, undertaken by the museums database project funded by the Office of Arts and Libraries revealed that every year they attracted 68 million visitors, a quarter of them tourists.

Table 5A   Attendances at public sector museums and galleries

| | Number of visitors (millions) | | | |
	1981	1983	1984	1985
National	16.5	15.8	16.9	17.6
Local authority	14.4	n/a	14.4	14.9

Source: Government Expenditure Plans, various years.

Table 5B   Attendances at national museums in 1986

	Numbers	% change from previous year
British Museum	3,869,639	-6.6
Imperial War Museum	1,175,834	-9.0
National Gallery	3,182,365	+0.8
National Maritime Museum	380,099	-36.6
National Portrait Gallery	624,520	+21.0
Science Museum	4,838,462	+5.0
Tate Gallery	1,153,355	+15.7
Victoria and Albert Museum	1,439,636	-30.4
Wallace Collection	170,797	-4.7
Merseyside Museums and Galleries	1,163,304	n/a
National Galleries of Scotland	529,675	-1.5
National Museums of Scotland	466,816	-34.2
National Museum of Wales	712,267	-6.7
Ulster Museum	295,683	
Ulster Folk and Transport Museum	161,036	

Source: Written answers, Hansard 19th January 1987, Cols. 394, 411/2, and 418, and information direct from the Ulster Museum and the Ulster Folk and Transport Museum.

Funding

Central Government funding to national museums is detailed in Table 6.

Table 6   Planned expenditure on national museums and galleries
                                             1987-88 (£ millions)

British Museum	13.938 (a)
Imperial War Museum	4.727 (a)
National Gallery	7.017 (a)
National Maritime Museum	4.677 (a)
National Portrait Gallery	1.899 (a)
Science Museum	9.589 (a)
Tate Gallery	6.497 (a)
Victoria and Albert Museum	11.680 (a)
Wallace Collection	0.939 (a)
Merseyside Museums and Galleries	9.414
Greater Manchester Museum of Science and Industry	1.252
Sir John Sloane's Museum	0.259
Museum of London	2.329 (b)
British Museum (Natural History)	17.558
National Museums of Scotland	5.017 (c)
National Galleries of Scotland	3.417 (c)
National Museum of Wales	12.504
Ulster Museum	2.657
Ulster Folk and Transport Museum	1.918
Ulster American Folk Park	0.681 (d)

Notes: (a) plus a share of the £50.006 million maintenance and
construction works undertaken by the Property Services Agency on
behalf of the Office of Arts and Libraries, approximately £30
million of which can be attributed to museums and galleries.
(b) Half the running costs of the museum, the other half being
met by the Corporation of the City of London.
(c) plus a share of the £7.493 million maintenance and
construction work undertaken by the Property Services Agency on
behalf of the Scottish Office, approximately £5 million of which
can be attributed to museums and galleries.
(d) An independent museum aided by the Northern Ireland Office.
Source: Supply Estimates 1987-88 and information supplied by the
Northern Ireland Department of Education.

Government help to local museums is principally given through
the Museums and Galleries Commission, the network of English Area
Museum Councils, and their Scottish and Welsh counterparts. The
planned expenditure of Commission is given in Table 7.

Table 7 Museums and Galleries Commission expenditure 1987-88(£m)

Grants to English Area Museum Councils	2.470
Grants to Museum Documentation Centre	0.120
Purchase Grants to local museums	1.282
Post-abolition funding	1.056
Other Grants	0.655
Running Costs	0.678

Source: Supply Estimates 1987-88

The first area museum council was established in the South West in 1959 and was quickly followed by others until, today, there are seven covering England plus separate councils in Scotland and Wales. As Table 8 shows, since they first received financial support in 1963 the amounts provided by the Office of Arts and Libraries and the Scottish and Welsh Offices has grown dramatically. Finance was initially intended to help with their operating costs but now goes largely to help fund individual museum projects, travelling exhibitions and other local initiatives.

Area museum councils are made up of representatives of museums and the organisations which run them, "with the objective of helping local museums to improve standards of care for their collections and service to the public. This is done by fostering and increasing co-operation, providing common services and information, and distributing government funds to approved projects."[19]

Table 8   Grants to area museum councils (£)

	England	Scotland	Wales	Total
1963/64	10,000			10,000
1965/66	14,000	2,000		16,000
1967/68	37,750	3,000	1,200	41,950
1969/70	52,000	3,000	1,250	56,250
1971/72	72,395	3,500	4,000	79,850
1973/74	120,000	4,460	7,500	131,960
1975/76	596,223	24,000	20,000	640,223
1977/78	900,000	100,000	31,831	1,031,831
1979/80	1,266,000	145,000	53,000	1,464,000
1981/82	1,631,546	197,000	126,533	1,955,079
1983/84	1,898,000	295,000	150,000	2,343,000
1984/85	2,194,400	276,000	205,355	2,486,355
1985/86(a)	3,291,000	581,000	230,000	4,102,000
1986/87(a)	4,531,000	650,000	280,000	5,461,000
1987/88(a)	4,758,000	655,000	300,000	5,713,000

Note: (a) These figures are not strictly comparable with earlier years. They include purchase grants to local authorities and, in the case of England, post-abolition funding. 1985/86 are actual expenditure while the latter two years are estimates.
Sources: Review of Area Museum Councils and Services and Supply Estimates 1987-88

Ancient monuments

The Historic Buildings and Monuments Commission for England was established under the 1983 National Heritage Act to take over many of the heritage functions of the Department of the Environment, along with the advisory responsibilities previously
----
[19] Review of Area Museum Councils and Services (London: HMSO 1984

exercised by the English Historic Buildings Council and Ancient Monuments Board. It manages 400 sites.

Attendance figures are only available for the 125 or so where an entrance charge is made and range from 655,690 at Stonehenge down to 144 at Thornton Abbey. The total number have risen from 3,889,800 in 1983 to a little over four million in 1985, producing an income of over two and a half million pounds a year.

The Department of the Environment remains responsible for the management of the Royal Palaces and Parks, several of which are open to the public. They attract over three and a half million visitors and raise over £10 million between admission charges and sales.

Elsewhere in the United Kingdom, responsibility for managing and maintaining publicly owned historic buildings and monuments has remained with the appropriate government departments.

In addition to maintaining the publicly owned heritage, the government possesses substantial powers to protect historic buildings and monuments in private ownership and contributes substantial sums towards their preservation. It receives advice in exercising its powers from a series of quangos such as the various Ancient Monument Boards, Historic Buildings Councils, and the Royal Commissions on Ancient and Historic Monuments.

Apart from the grants it pays directly to owners and to organisations such as the National Trust, it provides financial support through agencies such as the National Heritage Memorial Fund and the Redundant Churches Fund.

4. PUBLIC POLICY: The Underlying Problems

Against this background of diffuse development and widely scattered responsibility it is scarcely surprising that existing policies lack consistency. Admission to most national museums is free but some have compulsory charges and some have voluntary ones. The reverse is the case with major historic monuments. Some are free but most charge for admission.

The performing arts that come within the ambit of the Arts Council are heavily subsidised, many receiving half or more of their costs from the public purse. Those that fall outwith its scope receive little or no help.

This lack of consistency in existing practice is matched by a lack of clarity in both existing policy and the alternatives put forward to it by those active in the arts.

POLICY PROBLEMS

The stated aim of the government is "to encourage public access to, and enjoyment and appreciation of, artistic activity and the cultural heritage."[20] It is an ambition with which few supporters of the principle of public funding of the arts would disagree. And yet it raises some serious and important questions that are seldom if ever considered. What is it, for example, that the public are to be encouraged to enjoy and appreciate?

What is art?

Defining art is not a new problem. Virtually all studies of the arts begin by attempting to do so while, at the same time, admitting that art is fundamentally indefinable. Sir Ernst Gombrich, for example, wrote in his book, "The Story of Art", that "there is really no such thing as Art. There are only artists." And he warned that the very word, art, "may mean very different things in different times and places." [21]

Among those who make the attempt to define art, some seek narrow, traditional definitions that have the attraction of simplicity but exclude forms that might well, in subsequent generations, be accepted as art. Others choose the opposite extreme and adopt definitions that are so wide as to be practically useless.

Commenting on modern sculpture, for example, Marina Vaizey, art critic of the Sunday Times wrote "sculpture can be anything you
----

[20] The Government's Expenditure Plans 1987-88 to 1989-90 (Cm.56 London: HMSO 1987, Vol.2 page 211)
[21] Gombrich, E.H.: The Story of Art (New York: Phaidon Press, 1950)

like, so long as it is three-dimensional."[22]

Some Members of Parliament have graced House of Commons debates on the arts with such elusive concepts as "the spiritual capital of the nation" or "the invisible earnings of our minds" suggesting, perhaps, more a love of the sound of words than any desire to convey meaning.

The Arts Council recognises the problem. Its 1979 Annual Report stated that it had to "foster the best in the arts. The difficulty is that judgements about quality in the arts vary enormously, especially in contemporary arts which are breaking new ground, where one man's excellence may be another man's rubbish."[23]

The House of Commons Education, Science and Arts Committee decided, in their 1982 report not to attempt a definition of the arts but commended instead the definition contained in Public Law 209 of the 89th United States Congress setting up the National Foundation for the Arts and the Humanities, Section 3(b):

   "(b) The term 'the arts' includes, but is not limited to, music
   (instrumental and vocal), dance, drama, folk art, creative
   writing, architecture and allied fields, painting, sculpture,
   photography, graphic and craft arts, industrial design,
   costume and fashion design, motion pictures, television,
   radio, tape and sound recording, the arts related to the
   presentation, performance, execution and exhibition of such
   major art forms, and the study and application of the arts to
   the human environment."[24]

The government agreed with the committee that it was by no means easy to find an unequivocal and sufficiently comprehensive definition of 'the arts' and appeared to accept their use of the American definition.[25]

For national bodies, given the responsibility of spending public money to support the arts, this lack of a clear definition creates major problems. For a long time they avoided them by sticking to the narrow traditional view of art. More recently there has been a tendency towards the much wider, all-embracing perspective with the inevitable result that money is often spent in strange and incomprehensible ways.

Three "actors" receive a grant to march around the country with a
----
[22] Sunday Times, 5th October 1986
[23] 34th Annual Report and Accounts (London: Arts Council 1979,
     Page 6)
[24] Public and Private Funding of the Arts: 8th Report from the
     Education, Science and Arts Committee (HC 49, London: HMSO
     1982)
[25] Public and Private Funding of the Arts: Observations by the
     Government on the 8th Report from the Education, Science
     and Arts Committee 1981-82 (Cmnd 9172, London: HMSO 1984)

pole on their heads. £600 is paid to an "artist" who put together an empty sardine tin, a piece of sheet metal and a galvanised wash tub and claimed to have produced a meaningful statement about the sinking of the Belgrano. A lecturer received £6,000 to pay for cutting up the rotting remains of a ship on the mud flats at Canvey Island and then sewing them together again. A French "sculpture" received £23,000 for the crushed remains of two cars, valued by the equally artistic local scrap yard at about £6, the price at which they would willingly have produced any number of similar 'works of art.' The Tate Gallery displays a featureless pile of bricks while a submarine made out of old tyres graces the South Bank.

Newspapers delight in stories of such works being destroyed by lesser mortals who do not recognise them for what they are. Cleaners at the Royal Festival Hall, for example, swept up a work of art by Peter Fillingham and put it in the refuse skip, not recognising the artistic qualities that distinguished his collection of old helmets and graphite dust from the other dirt they were employed to remove. In their defense it has to be admitted that the artistic establishment at the pre-opening private viewing were also somewhat lacking in artistic appreciation and had themselves already trampled much of the graphite throughout the building.

Why art?

The lack of any clear cut idea of what is art is matched by the complete absence of any agreed view as to its function in society and why the government should encourage the public to enjoy and appreciate it.

For many years, there was an unquestioned general assumption on the part of politicians that art was somehow desirable in itself. Today that is no longer the case. Any debate on policy towards the arts now produces a wide variety of very different reasons for encouraging the arts.

Many people still look on the arts as something that is good for us and see artists as in some way superior people who bring enlightenment to their fellow men. Some argue that they have a vital educational role to play while others see them as simply offering a way to use increased leisure time.

All of them, however, fail to realise the implications of their attitudes. If the arts have the purpose they suggest, it makes little sense to insulate them through public subsidies from any necessity to attract the very public whose lives they are intended to benefit.

Those who see the arts purely as a business like any other whose output should be determined by public choice through the operation of market forces at least understand that what is in the end provided will be what the public wants and is willing to pay for.

Increasing numbers claim that the arts are important because they help to create a climate of awareness in which ideas can be more readily received. Art, they argue, mediates between the world as it is and the world as we would like it to be. Among them are a growing number who see art as a weapon legitimately to be used for the purpose of of social engineering.

Speaking in his former capacity as Shadow Minister for the Arts, for example, Norman Buchan stated that "we as socialists have always cherished the artist...because we recognise that artists provoke questioning, remove our blinkers, awaken compassion and fray at the nerve edge of our conciousness and awareness. Therefore, artists frequently set the agenda for which we as socialists can provide the ultimate answers. That is why we have a common purpose with artists...they emphasise the need for change even more clearly and sharply than the propagandists."[26]

Some local authorities have backed up this view by giving financial support to the work of radical political theatre groups. At an even more grass roots level, community arts groups have adopted a militantly left wing attitude, attacking the traditional subsidised arts as "bourgeois culture" and, as a writer in The Stage put it, "working to overthrow the State that enables it to work at all."[27]

At its best developed worst, this type of attitude to the arts is seen in Eastern Europe where the state determines what artists and what art are and are not politically acceptable.

In amongst the wide diversity of attitudes there are even those who do not seek to find any purpose but simply see art as a series of individual expressions by individual artists.

Achievement beyond measure

Begging the two questions what is art and why should it be supported, the government believes its policy of increasing access, enjoyment, and appreciation of the arts is achieved "by assisting the provision and development of the performing and visual arts; encouraging the arts to increase their income through better marketing and by attracting contributions from the private sector; maintaining and enhancing the national museums and galleries; helping to preserve objects of importance to the national heritage; and sustaining and developing national collections of literary material, archive and information stores."[28]

Here, the government do recognise that measuring success or failure is far from easy. In 1986, for example, they stated that "the value for money secured by the arts and libraries programme

----

[26] Hansard, 20th June 1986 Col.1310
[27] Quoted in the Arts Council's 1979 Annual Report (page 9)
[28] The Government's Expenditure Plans 1987-88 to 1989-90 (Cm.56 London: HMSO 1987, Vol.2 page 211)

cannot readily be quantified by final output measures."

They went on, however, to claim that it could be judged "by the quality, variety and comprehensiveness of the productions, exhibitions, scholarly work, loan and reference services provided by artistic bodies. The critical esteem with which the country's arts activities are received at home and abroad is also relevant, as is the evidence that they are a major factor in attracting tourism, and that growing private sponsorship and patronage reflect the value placed on the arts by the community."[29]

It is far from clear how quality, variety or comprehensiveness necessarily relate to public enjoyment and appreciation. Audiences attracted would seem to be a better measure. Table 9 does not suggest that any such correlation exists. Instead, the average numbers attending subsidised performances, except for the ballet, appear if anything to have declined.

Table 9   Seats sold for Arts Council aided performances

	1979/80	1980/1	1981/2	1982/3	1983/4	1984/5
Subsidised Theatre						
Performances	14,522	14,493	14,489	14,587	15,413	15,380
Seats sold (a)	5,265	5,523	5,119	5,118	5,533	5,557
Seats/performance	363	381	353	356	359	362
Subsidised Opera						
Performances	776	706	766	706	726	706
Seats sold (a)	1,099	1,021	1,094	993	995	986
Seats/performance	1,417	1,446	1,429	1,407	1,370	1,396
Subsidised Dance						
Performances	960	936	916	920	788	889
Seats sold (a)	1,037	1,023	950	1,013	908	1,013
seats/performance	1,080	1,093	1,038	1,101	1,153	1,140

Note: (a) seats sold in thousands
Source: Arts Council (from Facts About The Arts 2)

These figures do not suggest that any increase in critical acclaim has been echoed by the general public. Nor does it indicate any major impact on Britain's ability to attract tourists. As is discussed elsewhere in this report, that attraction lies largely in Britain's outstanding heritage, rather than in its subsidised performing arts.

Nor should the substantial increase in sponsorship be regarded as necessarily reflecting a raised value placed on the arts by the community. It is much more likely to be the result of a greatly increased awareness on the part of arts organisation of the potential it offers for raising money backed up by the financial encouragement offered through the Business Sponsorship Incentive Scheme.
----

[29] The Government's Expenditure Plans 1986-87 to 1988-89 (Cmnd. 9702 London: HMSO 1986, Vol.2 page 204)

In 1987, perhaps understandably, the government struck a more cautious note, warning that existing performance indicators do not "adequately reflect the full impact of programme expenditure" and suggesting that "the prestige attached to the country's arts activities at home and abroad is evidence of the high regard in which they are held."[30]

Why subsidy?

Fundamental to the whole structure of public policy towards the arts, however, is the post war assumption that the arts must be subsidised to survive. In view of its importance, the case for subsidies is dealt with separately in the following chapter.

The Price of Theatre Tickets and Hardback Novels

Each circle represents 25p

The above statistics indicate that over a period of 60 years the cost of a seat in the stalls is 5x as much as in 1910, the cost of a hardback novel is 14x as much, the cost of a bottle of whisky is 22x as much and 200 cigarettes 27x as much as their respective prices in 1910.

----

[30] The Government's Expenditure Plans 1987-88 to 1989-90 (Cm.56 London: HMSO 1987, Vol.2 page 214)

5. WHY PUBLIC SUPPORT?: Questioning the Unquestionable

Underlying public policy towards the arts is the presumption that they could not survive in an acceptable state without receiving continual support from the public purse. Without that perceived need, no public policy would be required.

Although some significant voices have questioned the desirability or effectiveness of subsidising the arts, they have been few and far between. When the House of Commons Education, Science and Arts Committee examined the funding of the arts in the early 1980s, for example, it received "no significant evidence against the basic principle of public support."[31] It was even prepared to state that "the Committee believe that the funding of the arts needs no justification beyond itself."[32]

Nonetheless, those who are sympathetic to the subsidised arts have felt it increasingly necessary in recent years to make a case for the continuation of public support. Their arguments are best summarised in the Arts Council's 1980 Annual Report by Sir Roy Shaw, the Secretary General of the Arts Council,[33] and in the Education, Science and Arts Committee's 1982 report.[34]

Because they have remained relatively unchallenged for so long it is worth examining those arguments in some detail.

LOW PRICE POLICY

The first argument put forward is that the arts have always received subsidies, from the church, the court, the aristocracy, and now the state. Because of this patronage, people have rarely paid the full price.

Quite apart from the fact that aristocratic patronage declined long before significant public subsidies started after the Second World War, this argument ignores the dramatic changes that have taken place in society, including both a substantial increase in real disposable incomes and a significant spread of wealth

Nonetheless, it is claimed that few people could afford to pay the full cost of attending the performing arts and that modern subsidies are designed to increase the accessibility of the arts to people throughout the country.

----

[31] Public and Private Funding of the Arts, 8th Report from the Education, Science and Arts Committee, Session 1981-82 (HC 49, London: HMSO 1982, Page lvi)
[32] Ibid. (Page xxxiii)
[33] 35th Annual Report and Accounts (London: Arts Council 1980, Pages 5-7)
[34] Ibid. (Pages lvi-lxxi)

It is a claim that is difficult to sustain in the light of the available evidence. Table 10 shows, for example, the composition of audiences at the Royal Opera House. Various surveys confirm that, after forty years of public subsidy, audiences for the arts still come overwhelmingly from the upper and middle classes.[35]

Table 10   Composition of Royal Opera House audiences 1980-81

Socio-economic group (U.K.)		London opera	London ballet	Manchester opera	Proms opera	Proms ballet
A	(3%)	30%	24%	29%	9%	11%
B	(11%)	36%	34%	38%	35%	24%
C1	(23%)	17%	17%	13%	23%	29%
C2DE)	(	3%	3%	3%	4%	5%
Students)	(64%) (	5%	10%	6%	23%	25%
Others)	(	9%	12%	11%	7%	5%

Source: Royal Opera House (table published in <u>Public and Private Funding of the Arts</u>)

Figure 1   Comparative prices, 1910 to 1977

Source: <u>34th Arts Council Annual Report and Accounts</u> (page 14)

[35] <u>Public and Private Funding of the Arts</u>, 8th Report from the Education, Science and Arts Committee, Session 1981-82 (HC 49, London: HMSO 1982, see page lxxxvii)

This failure to widen the audience for the arts is particularly significant when it is seen how far ticket prices have been held down compared with some other goods. Figure 1, published in the Arts Council's 1979 Annual Report, shows that, over sixty years, the cost of theatre tickets has increased by five times, much less sharply than books (fourteen times), alcohol (twenty-two times) or tobacco (twenty-seven times). In real terms they are cheaper now than they were before the First World War.

Not only has this relative price shift in favour of the theatre not changed the composition of audiences, it does not appear to have increased them significantly. In his last report in 1983, Sir Roy Shaw, admitted that "after over 30 years of Arts Council activity, the subsidised arts are patronised only by a minority; some put it as low as 2% of the population and no-one puts it higher than 10%." [36]

The assumption that there are a significant number of people who attend, or would like to attend, artistic events but cannot afford to pay the full price is further undermined by the evidence that even the smaller fringe groups and the "community arts", with their claim to closer links with the public, have not widened the audience for subsidised art. A survey conducted for the Arts Council and quoted in their 1979 report concluded that their audiences were "broadly similar to those found in most theatre audiences, i.e. largely middle class and with advanced formal education."[37]

It is clear that keeping the price of the subsidised arts artificially low has not provided an opportunity for the less well off in society to enrich their lives. It has largely served, instead, to allow those who traditionally enjoy the arts to do so more cheaply at the expense of the rest of society.

The arts are not alone

Another argument is that the arts are not unique in being insulated from the rigours of the market place. "The consumer has not been expected to pay the economic price for education, health services, or even for public swimming pools, amateur cricket facilities, public golf courses or public parks. All these services were exempted from the full impact of market forces because they were deemed essential to the quality of life in a civilised community."[38]

While it may be appropriate to compare the arts with amateur cricket, public swimming pools, golf courses or public parks, there must be few who would consider that they are as essential

----

[36] 38th Annual Report and Accounts (London: Arts Council 1983, Page 7)
[37] 34th Annual Report and Accounts (London: Arts Council 1979, Page 10)
[38] 35th Annual Report and Accounts (London: Arts Council 1983 Page 6)

to the quality of life as education or the National Health Service.

There is certainly a clear case for arguing that some goods and services in modern society are too important to be left to market forces alone: some parents would not, or could not, voluntarily educate their children; some people could not afford to meet medical bills; we could not have private, competing police or armies. But it must always be recognised that whenever the supply of any goods or services is determined in whole or in part by the state and funded through taxation, the power of the individual to control his own life and determine his own priorities is diminished.

In a free society, such state-controlled spending should be kept to the essential minimum with, where lack of purchasing power is seen to be a problem, some system of income support that leaves the individual with sufficient money to make his or her own choices. It is difficult to see how the subsidised arts -- or cricket grounds or golf courses -- could claim to be so different from other similar goods and services that they have to be treated in any special way.

Buying culture

The claim is then, of course, made that the operation of the market place is highly undemocratic since some voters have many more votes (i.e. more money) than others.

It is, of course, true that those with higher incomes will have a bigger influence in determining what the market provides. But it is equally true, as noted above and recognised by the Arts Council, that it is, and always has been, precisely those in the higher paid jobs who make up the overwhelming majority of the audiences for the subsidised arts. What subsidies mean in practice is that those, predominantly the lower paid, who do not patronise the arts are forced to pay for the pleasures of others who do. Far from the operation of the market place destroying their freedom of choice, it would actually enhance it by leaving more of their money in their pockets to spend as they please.

SUBSIDY OR INVESTMENT

An increasingly common argument is that public support for the arts should not be seen as a subsidy but rather as an investment. Kenneth Robinson, for example, writing as Chairman of the Arts Council, put forward the view that, "...money invested in the arts produces dividends of many sorts, not only in the social dividend of providing the citizen with richer leisure opportunities and generally enhancing the quality of life, but more tangible returns in stimulating tourism, contributing to the economy and raising our national prestige in the world."[39]
----
[39] 34th Annual Report and Accounts (London: Arts Council 1979, Page 4)

28

An official study of the economic benefits of the arts is currently under way but is not due to be published until later in 1987. Those who support subsidies to the arts have, however, already highlighted several areas where they claim public funding should be seen as an investment.

Nothing ventured

It is argued that subsidies are essential to fund arts which may initially please only a few, but subsequently reach far greater numbers through commercial theatre, film and television. Reference is made to the twenty or so productions that transfer each year from the subsidised to the commercial theatre.

It is further argued that the commercial arts depend on the subsidised ones for their people and ideas.

In doing so it is assumed that, in some unspecified way, the arts are totally different from all other forms of human enterprise. Other industries have to train their own workforce. Many other activities are far more expensive to develop to the point of profitability and yet the necessary money is found to finance them. Making the taxpayer fund the development of productions which will go on to make money for the commercial arts, and for those who produced them in the subsidised theatre, is impossible to justify.

It could be argued that the position is not quite so clear cut since only a fraction of productions each year go on to make money in the commercial sector. Companies in other areas of the economy, however, have to carry development costs where only a proportion of the work will ultimately prove profitable.

So far as the production of trained people and developed ideas is concerned, there seems no reason in principle why the commercial theatre, television or the film companies should expect to be treated totally differently from other businesses with their development cost carried by the taxpayer.

In similar vein, it is argued that the influence of "serious" art extends far beyond its immediate public. That, for instance, everyday design of furniture, fabrics, or of fittings has been revolutionised by the work of twentieth century visual artists whose work might once have seemed quite esoteric. Again, such an argument only makes the case for those who make a profit out of adapting art having to contribute towards the cost of producing the work they subsequently use.

While the Cork Report on the future of the theatre recognised the desirability of those who benefit from publicly supported artistic activity actually contributing towards its costs it, typically, suggested doing so through a statutory levy on the BBC and ITV, rather than through the operations of the market place where public preference might come into play.

Attracting tourists

It is in the area of tourism, however, that the biggest claims
are made. Subsidised arts are said to be a major attraction to
the tourists who spend £5.5 billion a year here.

In fact, against the 5.6 million people who in a year attend the
subsidised theatre, more than ten million go to plays in the West
End.

Nor are the arts alone in claiming credit for Britain's success
at attracting tourists. The British Tourist Authority, in written
evidence to the House of Commons Environment Committee stated
that "the importance of historic buildings and ancient monuments
for tourism cannot be stressed too highly." In their subsequent
oral evidence they added that "seventy percent of overseas
visitors, when we ask them why they came here and what they did,
say historic towns, cities and the heritage were the attractions
and the places they go to." [40]

Table 11 lists the top ten tourist attractions in 1985, none of
them recipients of Arts Council grants. Museums and galleries
attract many more visitors than the subsidised performing arts.
Over thirty-two million visited national and local authority
institutions while rather more than that attended independent
museums and galleries.

Table 11   Most visited historic properties and gardens in 1985
----

                                              number of visitors
----
Tower of London   2,430,323
Kew Gardens   1,112,177
Roman Baths and Pump Room, Bath   989,382
Edinburgh Castle   923,256
Royal Botanic Gardens, Edinburgh   820,387
Windsor Castle, State Apartments   735,000
Stonehenge   655,690
Warwick Castle   640,919
Hampton Court Palace   614,929
Beaulieu   551,879

Source: British Tourist Authority

Curiously, some of those who argue that public money put into the
arts is an investment also claim that it is justified because the
arts pay more in VAT than the government spends on the Arts
Council.

They no doubt hope that no-one will be uncharitable enough to
point out that they are comparing the VAT paid by all arts-
----
[40] Historic Buildings and Ancient Monuments: 1st. Report from
     the Environment Committee, Session 1986-87 (HC 146, London:
     HMSO 1987, Pages 259 and 266)

related activities, including the great majority that are profitable, with the subsidies paid to a small sector. It may not make much sense to tax people at the same time as giving them handouts, but the VAT paid by Arts Council clients constitutes only a tiny fraction of the money they get from it.

ARTISTIC INDEPENDENCE

Some argue that public subsidies are vital to protect the arts from over dependence on the market place; that those involved in producing art should not have to devote time and energy to raising money but should, instead, be free to concentrate on developing, innovating and planning their productions.

Dependence on attracting audiences, they claim, can lead to excessive commercialism at the expense of art. Dependence on sponsorship can create a kind of censorship in which nothing is produced which might offend the sponsor; in which risk and innovation are avoided.

These arguments are dealt with in greater detail elsewhere. It is only necessary to make the point here that the arts have no greater right than anyone else to be insulated from public opinion, whether expressed through the market place or through the political process.

Cheap jobs

It has even been argued that the arts merit public support because they can reduce unemployment more cheaply than any other form of government expenditure.

The argument, of course, ignores the fact that any money the state spends has to come out of the taxpayers' pockets. What jobs it might create will be matched by jobs lost elsewhere. If, however, money is to be spent in a vain attempt to increase employment then there are other areas, equally labour intensive, where the public might well consider the final product was of rather greater benefit than providing more artistic performances of the kind that they do not currently go to see.

International comparisons

Perhaps the weakest argument is that we should subsidise the arts because other countries do so to a greater degree than we do. Figures are quoted to show how much more is spent elsewhere in the world. Table 12 gives the figures quoted by the House of Commons Education, Science and Arts Committee in their 1982 Report. Somewhat conflicting figures are produced for six European countries in Facts About The Arts 2.[41]

----
[41]   Facts About The Arts 2 (London: Policy Studies Institute
        1986, Page 72)

31

Table 12   Public expenditure on the arts in nine countries

                                    $ per head   year

Austria   15.48   1981
Denmark   11.80   1977-78
France   12.37   1980
West Germany   38.80   1981
Netherlands   16.51   1979
Norway   19.91   1972
Sweden   24.91   1980-81
UK   7.74   1979-80
USA   0.71   1981

Source: Public and Private Funding of the Arts, page lxx

It is not, however, made clear quite why those countries that pay
higher subsidies should be the model rather than those, like the
USA, that pay substantially less and encourage private support
through offering tax incentives.

Self defence

In a final defence of their position, used more often to counter
possible cuts, it is claimed that "there are many other areas of
public expenditure which could more readily be pruned, because
expenditure there is far greater than on the arts, and there is
therefore scope for economies which would not destroy the
service."[42]

It is, of course, true that the budget of the Office of Arts and
Libraries is small in relation to other government departments.
That, in itself, is not an argument for giving it some sacrosanct
status. No area of public expenditure, however small it may be,
can expect to enjoy permanent immunity from examination, either
as to the continuing relevance of its objectives or to the degree
to which it succeeds in meeting them.

In fact, the Arts Council itself has to make precisely such
judgements between competing claims on the funds it has
available. Only the year before, for example, it withdrew its
support from The New Review as a result of which the magazine
ceased publication. No doubt the aggrieved editors could equally
have argued that the amount saved was tiny in relation to other
areas where cuts could have been made. They might even have
quoted from the Arts Council's own Annual Report: "Because of
their small readership, the cost of subsidising literary
magazines may seem disproportionate, but it can hardly be denied
that their continued existence is necessary to the health of our
literature.[43]
----
[42] 35th Annual Report and Accounts (London: Arts Council 1980,
     Page 6)
[43] 34th Annual Report and Accounts (London: Arts Council 1979,
     Page 25)

32

The Arts Council, of course, regularly reviews both its own operations and those of its clients. It is currently engaged in examining its own administrative costs and those of the regional arts associations.

They can hardly argue that the government, as custodians of the public purse, are not entitled to do the same.

THE CASE AGAINST SUBSIDIES

Nor, in the debate over public support, should it be forgotten that there are powerful arguments against the payment of subsidies.

The fundamental objection that money taken in taxes or rates and spent by the state reduces the individual's power over his or her own life, that it replaces consumer power with political and bureaucratic power, has already been noted above. It is a power that can all too readily be misused or abused for political ends.

It must also be recognised that subsidies lead to unfair competition. The heavily subsidised South Bank complex, for example, is already seen as a threat by other, less subsidised or fully commercial competitors.[44]

The commercial sector suffers, too, because the public compares their prices with those that are subsidised. At its most extreme, independent museums that charge have to work even harder to attract visitors accustomed to the free admission their public rivals offer.

But the saddest side effect is the way in which permanent subsidies create an attitude of total dependence on the state. In place of attempts to attract and satisfy the public, efforts are, instead, devoted towards encouraging a favourable attitude among those responsible for dispensing state patronage.

Forty years of state subsidies have led all too many people in the arts world to believe that they are entitled to public support as of right. And that attitude extends from the top of the Arts Council to the lowliest recipient of local authority funding.

It has created a clear yet artificial and unnatural demarcation line between what is recognised as "art" and what is not. It has produced a non-commercial elitism that takes pride in its unprofitability, indeed that despises artistic activities that pay as being corrupted by commercialism.

And that effect spills over into the non-subsidised arts who are beginning to feel that they too should enjoy some of the support they see their less popular competitors receiving.
----
[44] See, for example, the article by Robert Hewison in the Sunday Times of 15th March 1987. (Page 55)

The backing the subsidised stage receives, for example, is not universally welcomed by its commercial counterpart.

Comedian Johnny Beattie, speaking at the Scottish Civic Entertainment Association's 1986 Conference complained of "theatrical apartheid" and asked: "Is it right that the great mass of the population should be denied the sort of theatre that they like. Is it right that variety should be denied just because there is a small but highly articulate and vociferous minority who can blow their case into the ears of those who control the purse strings that what they like is art...is art...is art...and must be subsidised?"[45]

The existence of subsidies encourages a negative attitude to fund raising or proper pricing. Firstly, because it becomes assumed that the state will provide and, secondly, because success at fund raising, whether from customers or sponsors, is taken as a sign of less need for public support. In the case of the national museum and galleries the system of financing has now been changed but for the rest of the subsidised arts the position still remains that poverty prior to the annual award of grants is a useful negotiating position.

----
[45] Reported in The Scotsman of 9th October 1986

6. RAISING MONEY: The neglected art

Apart from public sector subsidies, the arts and heritage receive their income from a variety of sources, the principal ones being ticket sales, trading income and sponsorship or patronage. Table 13 gives a breakdown of the sources of income in 1983/84

Table 13   Sources of income 1983/4 (percentages)

	Earned income	Public support	Sponsorship & patronage
Professional performed arts			
National drama companies	46	53	1
English repertory companies	48	50	2
Indep. Theatre Council companies	28	70	2
Dance companies	34	62	3
Scottish repertory companies	40	56	4
Opera companies	33	60	7
Contract orchestras	41	52	7
London orchestras	71	17	12
English amateur organisations			
Music clubs	60	23	17
Music societies	49	17	34
Museums and galleries(a)			
National	7	93	
Local authorities	10	90	

Note: (a) The figures for museums and galleries are not strictly comparable with those in the rest of the table as no accurate information is available about their private resources.
Source: Facts About The Arts 2 (Table 1:43)

SETTING A PROPER PRICE

It is a long established practice of arts organisations to set their admission prices below any level at which they could realistically hope to cover their costs, expecting that the public purse will make up the difference.

In 1985, for example, Aberdeen District Council organise an "Alternative Festival" featuring folk music, jazz and a fiddlers rally, all traditionally commercially viable art forms. They provided a subsidy of £60,000 towards the expenses of the festival and still set their ticket prices at levels where even with every seat sold they would show a loss. In this case, the Arts Council declined to cover this deliberately planned deficit.

Nor is it just local government that plans to make a loss. The

Liverpool Royal Philharmonic Orchestra claimed that it was able to attract audiences of 90% capacity, both in the city and when on tour. And yet it needed more than half a million pounds from the Arts Council and was threatened with bankruptcy when the abolition of the metropolitan counties meant an end to its £421,000 grant from the Merseyside Metropolitan County Council. Only special transitional funding arrangements saved it.

Currently, opera is playing to packed houses across the country and yet is facing severe financial difficulties.

The various arguments that underly this attitude to pricing have been dealt with in some detail above. Unfortunately, they are often reinforced by the artistic attitude that putting on an excellent performance is the sole aim. Funding is regarded as secondary and within it the predominant effort is aimed at acquiring public funds. Some even regard taking a commercial view as an unacceptable intrusion into the perceived purity of artistic creativity.

The price of preservation

The position in public sector museums and galleries is even worse. The long established tradition of free admission has meant an almost total dependence on handouts from the public purse.

Yet charging for admission to Britain's heritage is nothing new or unusual. The vast majority of independent museums impose admission charges to help cover their costs. Stately homes, whether privately owned or held by the National Trust, charge their visitors. So, too, do 125 of the 400 historic sites administered by the Historic Monuments Commission on behalf of the Government. Their four million visitors pay £1.85 million in entrance fees and £0.72 million from other sales.

The Department of the Environment covers almost half of its costs in maintaining the Royal Palaces and Parks through charging the three and a half million people who each year visit the six royal palaces open to the public.[46] As Table 14 shows, they pay over £8 million in admission charges and spend a further £2 million on other facilities.

Among the national museums, the National Maritime Museum at Greenwich introduced compulsory admission charges some years ago. The Victoria and Albert Museum introduced its "voluntary" entry payments in 1986. Both expect to raise half a million pounds per year. The Science Museum introduced charges early in 1987.

Even the church is increasingly seeking income from those who come to see its historic buildings and its treasures. In the nineteenth century it was almost universal to charge for
----
[46]   Tower of London, Hampton Court Palace, Kensington Palace, Kew Palace, the Banqueting House, and, in those three years, Osborne House.

admission to cathedrals but, in the 1920s, such charges were gradually abolished. Over the past ten years they have started to reappear.

Table 14   Visitors and their expenditure at the Royal Palaces

	1983	1984	1985
Number of visitors	3,047,000	3,286,000	3,499,000
Admission receipts	£6.372m	£7.195m	£8.016m
Sales receipts	£1.245m	£1.437m	£2.127m
Income per visitor	£2.50	£2.63	£2.90

Source: Department of the Environment Memorandum included Historic Buildings and Ancient Monuments, 1st. Report from the Environment Committee, Session 1986-87 (HC 146, HMSO London 1987)

The church has long raised money from visitors, whether through voluntary collecting boxes and fabric funds in small parish churches or through the million pound fund raising appeals to save mediaeval cathedrals. Today, Ely Cathedral levies a charge on adults of £1.50 (£1 for the elderly, students and the unemployed). Some like Lincoln and Salisbury operate a system of voluntary charges while others make charges for visiting parts of the cathedral or ancillary buildings.

Charges are made for many of the special exhibitions that museums and galleries put on. In the case of the National Museum of Photography, Film and Television in Bradford, admission is free but a charge is made to attend showings of films in the IMAX cinema. They bring in over £400,000.

Indeed, it is worthy of note that bodies such as the Royal Academy and the Glasgow Royal Institute of Fine Arts were able to organise profitable exhibitions in the nineteenth century, often attracting larger numbers of paying visitors than they are able to do today.

It is scarcely surprising, therefore, that government's modest encouragement to national institutions to introduce charges by allowing them to retain any money they raise for their own use has aroused little protest from the man in the street.

Over the year 1986/87, the Minister for the Arts only received six letter on the subject of charges while the Secretary of State for Education and Science only thirty. Eighteen of them were from Members of Parliament.[47]

Why higher charges

Providing services at less than their full cost, indeed, in the extreme case, providing them free, has undesirable side effects.

----

[47] Written answers: Hansard 6th February 1987 (Col. 846), 5th March, 1987 (Col. 643) and 9th March, 1987 (Col. 21)

The less dependence there is upon the money that customers voluntarily pay, the less the wishes and preferences of those customers will be taken into account.

If what is produced does not in some way have to depend on direct public support through ticket sales or admission charges then it is unlikely to be directed at that public. The artistic wishes of the producers will hold sway, modified only by the need to obtain state support. Instead of energy being devoted to attracting potential customers it will be aimed at persuading potential benefactors, be they local councils or arts funding bodies.

If the arts and heritage are intended to be appreciated by the public, there has to be some pressure upon them to arouse the interest of people. That pressure is at its greatest when their full cost have to be met from the public as consumers, rather than the public as taxpayers or ratepayers.

If that means some forms of art have to change to survive it can only mean that they are currently failing to meet the essential requirement to interest the public and persuade them of the worth of their product. If it means they have to devote some energies towards attracting the public then that should be seen as a benefit, not a distraction. The need to attract audiences is recognised, even among those who advocate increased public funding. "To fund a performing company which had consistently little success in attracting the public would be a perverse use of public subsidy."[48]

It will be argued that increasing the cost of admission would have to be matched by increasing commercialisation of the arts; that, otherwise, attendances would decline leading to a loss of income rather than an increase. It is certainly true that introducing charges in some of the national museums has led to a fall in numbers. Attendances at the National Maritime Museum dropped by 36% and at the Victoria and Albert by 40%. No-one used to receiving a service free can immediately be expected to welcome the need to pay.

It must, however, be recognised that the commercial theatre, the independent museums and the great bulk of cultural activity that takes place without the benefit of state subsidies does so by charging realistic prices and persuading enough people that what they have to offer is worth paying for.

Indeed, it is more than likely that realistic charges, coupled with proper marketing, would do more to widen the circle of those who enjoy the arts and heighten their appreciation of them than two centuries of free museums and forty years of subsidised art have so far achieved.

Not all income has to come from the immediate consumer, however.
----
[48] 36th Annual Report and Accounts (London: Arts Council 1981, Page 6)

38

Given the right attitudes, there are many other ways in which the proceeds from ticket sales and admission charges can be supplemented so that the full cost does not have to be met.

PATRONAGE AND SPONSORSHIP

Individuals and businesses have patronised the arts over very many years. Outstanding recent examples include the gift by John Paul Getty Jr of £50 million to the National Gallery, the decision by the Sainsbury family to finance its new extension, and the £6 million from the Clore Foundation towards the new building at the Tate Gallery to house the Turner Collection.

The British Film Institute raised £5 million from private sources for the construction of its museum of the moving image on the South Bank and £3 million towards the cost of a new conservation centre for the National Film Archive.

Literature benefits from a growing number of privately funded awards and prizes for works of both fiction and non-fiction.

Although normally associated with specific projects, such support can take many forms. Fine Art auctioneers, Christies, are involved in providing courses in the decorative arts in both Glasgow and London, The John Lewis Partnership subsidises the purchase of tickets to arts events for their staff, while the car spares company, Unipart, provided a £10,000 prize for an "original sculpture" so long as it was made from car exhaust pipes and fittings.

Governments have traditionally encouraged personal charitable giving by allowing tax relief on seven year covenants. Further encouragement has recently been given by reducing the minimum duration of covenants to four years and through the introduction, in the 1986 Finance Act, of the scheme for "payroll giving" which allows tax deductable gifts to be made to charities by direct deduction from employees' pay. Advice is given to arts organisations on ways to exploit these opportunities.

Single donations by companies can now qualify for tax relief.

Sponsored growth

It is in the area of business sponsorship, however, that there has been the greatest recent growth in private financing of the arts. Significant giving started in the late 1960s and has accelerated rapidly in recent years as Table 15 shows.

It has been actively encouraged since 1976 by the privately formed Association for Business Sponsorship of the Arts. It receives limited financial support from the government and other support, since 1980, from the government's Committee of Honour for the Sponsorship of the Arts.

Table 15	Business Sponsorship of the arts (£millions)
1875-76	0.5
1977-78	3.0
1980-81	6.0
1982-83	13.5
1985-86	20.0
1986-87	25.0

Source: Association for Business Sponsorship of the Arts

Further important encouragement has been provided through the Business Sponsorship Incentive Scheme, established in 1984 to encourage sponsorship by matching the money raised from new private sources, pound for pound, from the tax payer. Smaller matching payment are made where existing sponsorship is significantly increased. Payments in either circumstances are limited to a maximum of £25,000.

In its first year the scheme brought in £4 million of new money and, by 1987 had produced over £11 million for the arts (£3 million of it from the government). 400 businesses had sponsored the arts for the first time and 250 existing sponsors had increased their support. It has been announced that the scheme is to be continued for a further year to 1988/89.

Sponsorship takes a variety of forms. The 1986 Commonwealth Arts Festival, held in Edinburgh to coincide with the Commonwealth Games, attracted sponsorship including a £300,000 package from Rank Xerox.[49] The Scottish Postal Board commissioned a new work by composer Edward Harper with a post code built into the title. The Chamber Orchestra of Europe was given free advertising by an existing sponsor, The Economist, to seek new sponsors.

Faced with the loss of funding due to the abolition of the GLC, Sadler's Wells theatre was able to attract sponsorship of £50,000 from Northern Telecom and £175,000 over two years from the Digital Equipment Company.[50] The Business Sponsorship Incentive Scheme added £25,000 of taxpayers' money to that.

The most generous sponsors are the banks and oil companies with insurance, transport, newspapers, television and the alcohol industry becoming increasingly prominent. Trade unions, however, have begun to enter the field. A tour by the 7:84 Theatre Group and Wildcat featuring a play about social service cuts was partially funded by a £20,000 grant from Nalgo.

----

[49] Backing from public sources, however, included £100,000 from the Foreign and Commonwealth Office, £25,000 from the Scottish Arts Council and £10,000 from the City of Edinburgh District Council and very substantial support in kind through the provision of council property and facilities.

[50] The money from the Digital Equipment Company was part of a half a million pound package covering a whole range of dance activities.

The Association for Business Sponsorship of the Arts describes sponsorship as a "mutually advantageous liaison between business and the arts for the ultimate good of the whole community." [51]

It is not a view that is universally shared.

Some argue that dependence in any way on sponsorship creates a kind of censorship in which nothing is produced which might offend the sponsor; others that risk and innovation are avoided. Some, drawing on American examples of sponsors "interfering" with television scripts or plots, have expressed the fear that the growth of commercial sponsorship might lead, some day, to scripts being amended to include particular brand names or even paintings including specific named products.

Those who champion the minority arts and the radical theatre complain that sponsors are only interested in established arts and will not back new work of unproven public appeal or merit.

Most sponsorship money does, indeed, currently go to the larger established organisations with a good and predictable box office appeal, usually to support performances of one sort or another. The visual arts find it difficult to raise sponsorship money.

It should be borne in mind, however, that it is not beyond the wit of arts organisations to rearrange their finances so that income from sponsorship of their popular activities released money that could then be used for the less popular or more adventurous work.

The warning that theatres will not put on plays that offend potential sponsors highlights one danger of outside funding. But those who put it forward ignore the equal danger that bodies responsible for public funding will also impose their own orthodoxy on the performing arts. Those that do not meet the criteria laid down must face the consequences of displeasing their paymasters. The restraints need not be political or social, as the flourishing radical political theatre shows, but they will certainly exist.

The growth of sponsorship has exceeded the expectations of some among the arts community. In 1981, the then Minister for the Arts, Lord Gowrie, stated that "over a period of years I do not think that there is a chance of substantially increasing" sponsorship.[51] Since then it has more than doubled.

There is no reason to assume that such pessimism would be any more justified today. In the United States, where tax incentives have long been available to encourage company donations, 1.5% of pre-tax profits are used for donations, around a quarter of it going to the arts. In the UK, corporate giving amounts to only

----

[51] Public and Private Funding of the Arts, 8th Report from the Education, Science and Arts Committee, Session 1981-82 (HC 49, HMSO London 1982, Page cii)

0.2% of pre-tax profits.

There is obviously still tremendous scope for arts and heritage organisations to increase their income from business sources.

OTHER INCOME

Virtually all arts organisations enjoy further opportunities to raise additional money, including sales of publications, running or franchising shops, restaurants and other trading ventures, making charges for specialist services to the public or other institutions, providing and charging for educational facilities, or simply letting out premises.

Few, however, pursue those opportunities with sufficient enthusiasm, partly because success was often rewarded in the past by equivalent reductions in public subsidies and partly from a common feeling that fund raising detracts from their main purpose.

Penalising successful fundraising is something the present government have explicitly rejected in its recent changes in the way national museums are funded. It is something it should ensure is common policy throughout its own operations and those of the various agencies and other bodies it uses to support arts and heritage activities.

Arts organisation must change their attitudes, too, and recognise the benefits, particularly in greater freedom of action, that raising their own income brings. Instead of complaining that "many artistic directors have to spend too much of their time worrying about money or wooing possible business sponsors to the detriment of their artistic role",[52] they should follow the example of institutions like the National Maritime Museum which appointed a Head of Marketing with responsibility for "constant monitoring of all our receipts with a view to deriving maximum benefit from every aspect of the Museum's activities."[53]

Over the past two years, such extra income raised by the English national museums has increased from around 8% of running costs to nearly 11%. A breakdown by institution is given in Table 16.

In lieu of tax

A further way in which governments help conserve the nation's heritage is through the acceptance of works of art, buildings or estates in settlement of tax debts.

----

[52] 38th Annual Report and Accounts (London: Arts Council 1983, Page 10)
[53] Letter from the museum's director, published as part of the Minutes of Evidence to the House of Commons Education Science and Arts Committee (HC 367 London: HMSO 1986)

Table 16   Proportion of running expenses raised privately

                         Grant in aid   Own income   % running
                             (£)   (£)   costs

British Museum   13,938,000   1,853,000   11.73
Imperial War Museum   4,727,000   1,259,000   21.03
National Gallery   7,017,000   144,000   2.01
National Maritime Museum   4,677,000   460,000   8.95
National Portrait Gallery 1,899,000   726,000   27.66
Science Museum   9,589,000   1,950,000   16.90
Tate Gallery   6,497,000   342,000   5.00
Victoria and Albert Museum 11,680,000   625,000   5.08
Wallace Collection   939,000   57,000   5.72

Source: Supply Estimates 1987-88

£2 million a year is specifically set aside for such acceptance in lieu of tax, and this sum is backed up by a further contingency sum of £10 million provided by the Treasury. It was that contingency which allowed the acquisition of Constable's "Stratford Mill".

Over the past ten years some significant acquisitions for the nation have taken place in this way. Apart from "Stratford Mill", now hanging on public display in the National Gallery, earlier outstanding acquisitions have included Bellini's "Madonna and Child", now in the Ashmolean Museum, Godman's collection of Islamic Pottery, now in the British Museum and Calke Abbey and grounds handed over to the National Trust.

Such acceptances are generally associated with taxes on capital where substantial unforeseen liabilities can arise. There seems no reason, however, why the scheme should not be developed into a more general system that replaced part, at least, of the existing framework of public subsidies by allowing companies and individuals to pay a restricted percentage of their tax bill in the form of support to arts and heritage organisations, whether it be through donations of works of art, contributions to construction costs or in some other way.

Such a scheme, relying on the individual decisions of widely differing organisations and individuals, could be beneficially used to encourage the purchase of work by present day painters and sculptures who have all too often received little or no support from the present system.

7. ARTISTIC INDEPENDENCE: The Way Forward

The traditional view of the arts lobby and their political allies is that the answer to all their problems is more public money and more government involvement. The Government itself makes a virtue of increasing its financial support while both the Labour Party and the Alliance have stated their view that public funding for the Arts should be doubled and that an all embracing Ministry should be established with responsibility for the entire range of arts and related matters.[54]

The Labour Party have proposed a statutory obligation on local authorities to provide for the arts, entertainment and museums with each council publishing plans for the development of arts in their areas. It has suggested that the Arts Council should be directly elected from the regions and the arts themselves in order for it to become a powerful voice representing the arts to the minister.[55]

Despite forty years of evidence to the contrary, the belief still remains that continuing and increasing public support for the arts might yet widen their appeal and make them attractive to the majority of the public. It is still not even recognised that the very act of providing subsidies reduces the need to attract the public and that any increase in those subsidies can only reduce that need even further.

If the aim is, as the government states, "to encourage public access to, and enjoyment and appreciation of, artistic activity and the cultural heritage"[56] then it is time to recognise that present policies, particularly those relating to the arts, are not achieving that objective. It is time to recognise that public subsidies are the problem, not the solution.

"It must surely be patent to all," wrote John Osborne, "that subsidised theatre -- parasitic, overbearing, wasteful, a bureaucratic powerhouse and refuge for mediocrity and graft -- is not merely inimical to the authentic creative spirit, but is at perfect odds with the once independent English character that begs no State favours or the approval of self-esteeming jacks-in-

----

[54] "The next Labour Government will...bring together not only arts and libraries, museums, galleries and crafts, but bring with them publishing, photography, film, press, video, satellite and radio in one unified ministry for the arts and media." Mark Fisher, Shadow Minister for the Arts (Hansard 12th March 1987 Col. 504)

[55] See Norman Buchan, speaking as Shadow Minister for the Arts, Hansard 20th June 1986 (Cols. 1309-10)

[56] The Government's Expenditure Plans 1987-88 to 1989-90 (Cm.56 London: HMSO 1987, Vol.2 Page 211)

office."[57]

Cutting the ties

Though phasing out state subsidies may be essential if the performing arts are to have a healthy and independent future, decades of growing dependence on state subsidies will not be easily or quickly ended. Organisations which depend on the state for half or more of their income, even were they to welcome the challenge of seeking self-sufficiency, will not be able to adjust overnight. Artistic establishments who have not been noted in the past for encouraging entrepreneurial skill, even under severe financial pressure, will need time to change their attitudes.

But any transitional phase should be as short as possible. The arts lobby is nothing if not articulate and will be vehement in its opposition. Failures in the past to raise subsidies by more than the rate of inflation has been enough to provoke outrage.

Some organisations will find the transition easy to make. Some have audiences that are large enough and buoyant enough to carry significant increases in ticket prices. Some will find it possible to increase their audiences. Some will be able to tap the continuing potential for patronage and sponsorship. Some will be able to exploit the many opportunities for ancillary sales and fund raising. Some will be able to streamline their operations and reduce their overheads.

Even Covent Garden which receives the biggest subsidies of any artistic organisation should not find it impossible to attain self-sufficiency. Quite apart from its own development plans, currently under discussion, a report, produced privately at a cost of £25,000 by the former chief executive of the Maples furnishing group, put forward fifty detailed proposals to exploit the Royal Opera House's reputation. In total, they were capable of generation £10 million a year.[58]

Some, however, will find financial independence difficult to attain and there will inevitably be those who find that all their efforts, however sincerely made, cannot bridge the gap between their operating costs and the money the public is willing to pay.

The most sensible way forward would, therefore, be to adopt a three- or four-year programme over which the Arts Council's grant would be reduced to zero. With their detailed knowledge of their clients' strengths and weaknesses they would be able to phase individual reductions, taking into account areas where cuts in subsidy could be made quickly and those where more time would be required.

----

[57] "The shabby end to a theatrical dream", The Observer, 6th July 1986
[58] See "Stony ground at the Garden" in The Sunday Times, 18th January 1987.

45

Towards the end of such a transitional period it would be possible to assess how many, if any, arts organisations were unlikely to be able to survive. A decision could then be made as to whether they were of sufficient merit or importance to be worth retaining.

If any were, they could, of course, continue to receive public subsidies. Far better, however, would be to break the links with the state. In return for adopting charitable, non-profit making status with restrictions on the levels of salaries that they could pay, such organisations could be offered either relief from VAT or the provision of an endowment, sufficient to cover their anticipated annual losses.

The other arts

Though small in relation to the support given to the performing arts, significant Arts Council money goes to support other activities such as writing and publishing, film making, and the purchase and display of paintings and sculpture.

The Arts Councils and the Regional Arts Associations between them spend roughly £1.5 million supporting literature of one form or another.[59] A small amount goes to give grants to writers but most goes to support literary magazines, small specialist publishers, the National Book League, the Poetry Book Society and the Poetry Society. Help was given in 1985/86 to establish a poetry book distribution service.[60]

In relation to the publishing industry the amounts involved are trivial and it is difficult to see why immediate steps should not be taken to seek the transfer of all these activities into appropriate private hands. Private publishers have a long history of supporting work which they recognised had merit but thought unlikely to prove profitable.

It could well be, however, that much that is currently subsidised would, in fact, prove profitable in the right hands. The poetry book distribution service with only two representatives, for example, achieved sales of £100,000 in its first year. Some of the Poetry Society's readings attract substantial audiences. The Arts Council's 1986 Report mentions one at the Queen Elizabeth Hall which attracted over 1,000 people and another in the Lewisham Town Hall for which 850 tickets were sold.[60]

Arts Council involvement in film, video and broadcasting activity is largely concerned with the production of arts related documentary and educational material. Many are co-productions with the BBC or the independent television companies or receive financial support from them. Occasionally, overseas broadcasting interests are involved. Some support with educational work comes

----

[59] Written Answer, Hansard 12th January 1987
[60] 41st. Annual Report and Accounts (London: Arts Council 1986, Page 19)

from another quango, the British Film Institute.

There seems no reason, in fact, why these activities should not be transferred to the other agencies and organisations already involved. The production of films for television, for example, should surely be financed by the stations which propose to show them, not the taxpayer.

Around £5 million is spent promoting the creative arts through exhibitions and displays of existing and new art in national, local and private galleries. In addition, the Arts Council tries to encourage public bodies to commission or buy works of art for display on or in their buildings.

Buying and displaying the work of new artists is, perhaps, the most constructive way those active in the creative arts can be given support. Public bodies have certainly played their part in the past and should be encouraged to do so in the future. But so, too, should commerce, industry and other private bodies. Some have a commendable record of commissioning work but many have not.

The suggestion has been made that there should be a legal requirement that one percent of the cost of constructing new buildings should be used to commission works of art for inclusion in or on the building. Quite apart from the undesirability of introducing even more compulsions into our already highly regulated society, there is no guarantee that such a scheme would achieve the desired result. There would be problems in defining what was or was not acceptable as "art" under such a scheme and much of the work commissioned would be treated as a legal necessity rather than as something with its own intrinsic merit. If work of quality were obtained it would be as much by accident as design.

A better option would be to provide a tax incentive as discussed elsewhere in this report. While there would still be difficulties of definition, work would at least have been commissioned because it was wanted, not because the law of the land required it.

The display of existing art raises rather different principles, more akin to those raised by museums and galleries. They are discussed in the following paragraphs.

FREEING THE HERITAGE

The benefits of independence from local and national government can clearly be seen among the rapidly growing number of independent museums and galleries.

In the first five years that National Heritage ran its "Museum of the Year" award, it was won each time by an independent museum. Over the fourteen years that the award has been made, no fewer than nine of the winners have been independents.

John Letts, the founder of National Heritage, is in no doubt why. "There is something about public fund support which sometime appears to have the effect of extinguishing initiative and merely encouraging pointless excess." He concluded that "initiative flourishes in independence."[61]

Similar views have been expressed by The Good Museums Guide. In their view "independent museums have done much better...than local authority museums," a fact they attributed to a "lacking in entrepreneurial spirit" on the part of the latter.[62]

The same point has been recognised in the public sector. Sir Roy Strong, then Director of the Victoria and Albert Museum, told the House of Commons Education, Science and Arts Committee that "...we have done too little asking (the public) what they want, and that does not mean going down to the lowest common denominator. We must follow the achievement of the highly successful private museums over the last few years and the whole change in presentation of historic houses."[63]

First steps

Over recent years, the government have taken a number of steps towards giving the national museums greater independence of action. Boards of Trustees have been appointed where they did not previously exist. The method of funding has been changed to allow greater flexibility and the retention for their own use of any extra money they raise. Control over the maintenance of its buildings is to be transferred to each institution.

It must be very doubtful, however, if any of the national museums and galleries could be expected to cover their entire operating costs from income they themselves generate. As Table 16 showed, only four are currently raising more than ten percent of their running costs and only two raise more than twenty percent. And those running cost do not include the expense of maintenance and construction.

Overall, the national museums under the control of the Office of Arts and Libraries spend just under £100 million a year and raise perhaps seven percent of that themselves. A more aggressive approach to marketing has already seen a significant overall rise in that proportion but the differences shown in Table 16 suggest that there is still considerable scope for raising yet more private income.

As an indication of the more aggressive approach to fund raising
----
[61] Letts, John: "More Initiative, More Money" contained in Raising Money for the Arts (London: Directory of Social Change 1978)
[62] Hudson, Kenneth: The Good Museums Guide (London: Macmillan 1982)
[63] Oral evidence included in Revised Financing Arrangements for the National Museums and Galleries (HC 367 London:HMSO 1986)

now being taken, it is worth quoting the Director of the National Maritime Museum, R.Ormond, who told the House of Commons Education, Science and Arts Committee that they were already well down the road of maximising their receipts having:

"(a) introduced admission charges some two years ago -- with no drop in the number of visitors; indeed, we are looking shortly to extend the museum's hours of opening;
(b) established a trading company (NMM Enterprises Ltd) to run the Museum's Bookshop with all the profits covenanted to the Museum;
(c) set up a Development Fund to enable corporate bodies to donate to, or directly fund, certain long term projects, and which we intend to launch publicly later this year;
(d) appointed a Head of Marketing whose responsibilities include constant monitoring of all our receipts with a view to deriving maximum benefit from every aspect of the Museum's activities."[64]

From the experience of the admission schemes operated by the National Maritime Museum and the Victoria and Albert Museum, and the obvious success of private museums, there seems no reason why there should not be a more widespread use of charges, raising at least £10 million and possibly substantially more.

Even with such efforts at fund raising, there will still be an unbridgable gap between the costs of running most museums and what they could realistically raise. It is estimated that every existing visitor would have to pay between £5 and £6 to cover the costs of maintaining local and national museums and galleries.[65]
Nonetheless, the benefits of independence to the institutions and the public they serve is so clear that the opportunity should be taken to build on the progress that has already taken place.

Sharing the burden

The most attractive option would be to replace each institution's grant with an endowment fund sufficient to produce an income equivalent to their expected annual deficit.

Setting up such funds, along with any that were required in the artistic field, would involve substantial sums of money. To fund the national museums, even allowing for a substantial increase in their other income, could involve something of the order of £800 million to a billion pounds.

There is, however, a readily available source for such funds. The government still have large holdings in the partly privatised
----
[64] Letter included in Revised Financing Arrangements for the National Museums and Galleries (HC 367 London:HMSO 1986)
[65] The Government's Expenditure Plans 1987-88 to 1989-90 (Cm.56 London: HMSO 1987, Vol.2 page 211)

industries such as British Telecom and the others. As the privatisation programme progresses, there will be more. It would be a simple matter to use some of those shares to provide endowments. The loss in dividend income to the Treasury would be matched by the savings in grants that were no longer paid.

There would be the added benefit that such shareholdings would assist in the government's policy of keeping control of these former nationalised industries in British hands.

Similar arrangements could be made to give the Historic Buildings and Monuments Commission for England greater independence in its role as custodian of its 400 historic sites. It could then charge the government for the advisory and other work it carries out. An endowment fund in this case might be no larger than £500 million to £600 Million.

If such changes are to be made, it would make sense for the Scottish, Welsh and Northern Ireland Offices to examine the opportunities for following the English example with regard to their historic houses and ancient monuments.

Bridging the gap

In parallel with the phased elimination of direct subsidies to the arts and the transformation of most national heritage bodies into totally independent institutions, substantial efforts should be devoted to encouraging increased private support for artistic activity and the preservation of the national heritage.

The government's Arts Marketing Scheme should be substantially strengthened so that arts and heritage organisations can receive the fullest possible advice and assistance in increasing their attendances and income.

The government should also use its influence, and if need be its powers, over the BBC and the independent broadcasting organisations to ensure that they come to reasonable arrangements for supporting those artistic activities from which they benefit. Such arrangements were reached in the recent re-organisation of public support for film making and the difficulties should not prove insurmountable.

More importantly, however, there should be a much more aggressive approach towards encouraging individual and company support for the arts. As already noted, corporate giving in the United Kingdom amounts to only 0.2% of pre-tax profits compared with 1.5% in the United States. Even a modest move towards American levels of giving could transform the fortunes of many arts organisations.

The success of the Business Sponsorship Incentive Scheme shows what can be achieved with limited government encouragement. It has yet to be seen how far the further steps, taken in recent budgets, to stimulate charitable giving will be similarly

50

exploited to the benefit of the arts.

Other possibilities that the government could adopt to increase private funding include widening the scheme for accepting works of art or parts of the national heritage in lieu of tax, increasing the tax allowances for charitable giving and introducing a tax check-off scheme. All depend, however, on the Treasury being willing to forego a larger part of its anticipated tax income.

Transferring taxes

Table 17 shows that taxes on income, profits and capital are expected to raise £59 billion in the coming year. The total from all forms of taxation is expected to be £117.5 billion. At present, only £3 million is specifically provided for accepting works of art in lieu of tax with a further contingency of £10 million available for use in special circumstances. No accurate estimates exist of the tax foregone as a result of donations to the arts under other schemes.

If a system were to be introduced that allowed any taxpayers to allocate up to 1% of their taxes to a charitable body of their choice, the potential benefits to the currently subsidised arts and heritage organisations could be dramatic. The loss in revenue from the introduction of such a scheme would be unlikely to reach £500 million. As Table 17 shows, such a sum is well within the range of error in forecasting the 1986/87 tax receipts.

Table 17		Revenue from selected taxes (£m)	
	1986 Budget	Latest Estimate	1987/8 Forecast
Income tax	38,500	38,300	39,900
Corporation tax	11,700	13,400	15,000
Petroleum revenue tax	2,400	1,260	1,680
Capital gains tax	1,050	1,050	1,300
Development land tax	35	55	20
Inheritance tax	910	990	1,100
Total	54,595	55,055	59,000
Income from all taxes	108,600	111,100	117,500

Source: Financial Statement and Budget Report 1987-88 (HC 194 London: HMSO 1987, Table 6B.3)

All initiatives aimed at encouraging private funding depend, however, on the willingness and enthusiasm of the arts and heritage organisations to exploit the opportunities offered. Their success or failure ultimately depends, as it rightly should, on their own efforts.

7. POSTSCRIPT: Politics or Progress?

It is clear that there are only two roads forward for Britain's arts and heritage. The one is to continue to depend on public support, always likely to be given grudgingly and with strings attached; always likely to be reduced in an economic crisis; always subject to changes in government; and always likely to carry with it the threat or the reality of political interference.

It was in the uncertainty of cross-party political support that Sir Roy Shaw foresaw potential disaster for the arts. His belief that it could be averted while still retaining substantial and growing public subsidies from the taxpayer defies all previous experience of the political process.

There is only one way to avoid becoming embroiled in political warfare and that is to be totally independent of government. It is towards such independence that this report concludes the arts and heritage should look.

Such independence offers a major challenge which some might not survive. Equally, and more importantly, it offers an opportunity; an opportunity to create a partnership with the majority of the public that forty years of subsidies has signally failed to achieve.

APPENDIX: The Quango Roll Call

As will be clear from this report, much of the government's involvement in arts and heritage matters is discharged directly through a series of quangos and indirectly through a wide range of other bodies which receive public funding.

The arts are principally supported through the various arts councils, their committees and the Regional Arts Associations covering England. There are a number of other bodies, however, with an involvement in arts matters such as the Advisory Committee on the Purchase of Works of Art or the Committee of Honour on Business Sponsorship of the Arts.

Heritage matters are the concern of a much larger number of administrative and advisory bodies from the Historic Buildings and Monuments Commission for England with four hundred properties under its control and a wide variety of other powers and responsibilities down to boards of trustees for individual museums.

The House of Commons Environment Committee, in its 1987 report, considered that "there could be a considerable degree of rationalisation among the statutory bodies which have grown up over the years."[65]

Beyond, are a whole range of independent bodies who receive financial support from the government such as the various branches of the National Trust and the Civic Trust.

The following list sets out those government sponsored bodies with some responsibility for the arts or the heritage.

A: Quangos directly responsible for arts or heritage matters(a)

Advisory Board for Redundant Churches (1969)
Advisory Committee on Historic Wreck Sites (1973)
Advisory Committee on the Purchase of Works of Art (1956)
Advisory Committee on Works of Art in the House of Commons
Advisory Council on the Export of Works of Art (1952)
 -- Reviewing Committee on the Export of Works of Art
Ancient Monuments Board for Scotland (1913)
Ancient Monuments Board for Wales (1913)
Arts Council of Great Britain (1945)
 -- Scottish Arts Council
 -- South Bank Board
 -- Welsh Arts Council
Arts Council of Northern Ireland (1943, renamed 1963)
British Council (1934)
British Film Institute
Committee of Honour on Business Sponsorship of the Arts (1980)
----

[65] Historic Buildings and Ancient Monuments, the 1st. Report from the Environment Committee, Session 1986-87 (HC 146 London: HMSO 1987)

53

Crafts Consultative Committee (1977)
Crafts Council (1971)
Design Council (1944)
Historic Buildings Council for Scotland (1953)
Historic Buildings Council for Wales (1953)
Historic Buildings and Monuments Commission for England (1985)
Museums and Galleries Commission (1931)
National Heritage Memorial Fund (1980)
Northern Ireland Historic Buildings Council (1973)
Northern Ireland Historic Monuments Council (1971)
Redundant Churches Fund
Reviewing Committee on the Export of Works of Art (1952)
Royal Commission on Historical Manuscripts (1869)
Royal Commission on the Ancient and Historical Monuments of England (1908)
Royal Commission on the Ancient and Historical Monuments of Scotland (1908)
Royal Commission on the Ancient and Historical Monuments of Wales (1908)
Royal Fine Arts Commission (1927)
Royal Fine Arts Commission for Scotland (1927)
Scottish Film Council (1934)(b)

B: Quangos with some responsibility for arts and heritage matters

British Tourist Authority (1969)
British Broadcasting Corporation (1926)
Council for Small Industries in Rural Areas (1968)
Development Board for Rural Wales (1977)
Development Commission (1909)
English Tourist Board (1969)
Highlands and Islands Development Board
Local Enterprise Development Unit (1971)
Scottish Tourist Board (1969)
Scottish Development Agency (1975)
Wales Tourist Board (1969)
Welsh Development Agency (1976)

Note: (a) The boards of trustees for individual national museums and galleries have not been listed.
(b) Now a standing committee of the Scottish Council for Educational Technology)